E $8.25

Lu   Lunn, Carolyn
        A buzz is part of
       a bee

DATE DUE

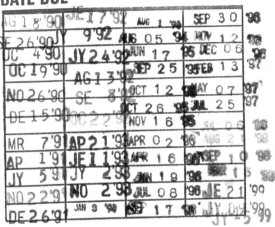

A BUZZ IS PART OF A BEE

By Carolyn Lunn

Illustrations by Tom Dunnington

Prepared under the direction of Robert Hillerich, Ph.D.

℗ CHILDRENS PRESS®
CHICAGO

LIBRARY OF CONGRESS
Library of Congress Cataloging-in-Publication Data

Lunn, Carolyn.
   A buzz is part of a bee / by Carolyn Lunn ;
illustrations by Tom Dunnington.
      p.   cm. — (A Rookie reader)
   Summary: Enumerates a series of words and the
greater things of which they are a part, such as leaf
and tree, elbow and arm, candle and cake, and tail and
kite.
   ISBN 0-516-02062-5
   1. Vocabulary—Juvenile literature. [1. Vocabulary.]
I. Dunnington, Tom, ill. II. Title. III. Series.
PE1449.L76   1990
428.1—dc20   89-25434
                                                 CIP
                                                  AC

A leaf is part of a tree.

A buzz is part of a bee.

A wheel is part of a skate.

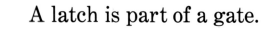

A latch is part of a gate.

A thorn is part of a rose.

A freckle is part of a nose.

An elbow is
part of an arm.

9

A barn is part of a farm.

A pea is part of a pod.

A hook is part of a rod.

Candles are part of a cake.

A handle is part of a rake.

A tail is part of a kite.

Dark is part of the night.

A lace is part of a shoe.

A keeper is part of a zoo.

A pit is part of a peach.

Sand is part of the beach.

Bubbles are part of a bath.
Stones are part of a path.

A caboose is part of a train.

Stripes are part of a cane.

A fish is part of the sea

29

and my shadow is part of ME!

WORD LIST

a	dark	me	sand
an	elbow	my	sea
and	farm	night	shadow
arm	fish	nose	shoe
barn	freckle	of	skate
bath	gate	part	stones
beach	handle	path	stripes
bee	hook	pea	tail
bubbles	is	peach	the
buzz	keeper	pit	thorn
caboose	kite	pod	train
cake	lace	rake	tree
candles	latch	rod	wheel
cane	leaf	rose	zoo

About the Author

Carolyn Lunn is an American, now living in England with her British husband and three-year-old son. As well as writing stories, she enjoys running, cooking, and gardening. Her other books include *A Whisper Is Quiet*, *Bobby's Zoo*, and *Purple Is Part of a Rainbow*.

About the Artist

Tom Dunnington divides his time between book illustration and wildlife painting. He has done many books for Childrens Press, as well as working on textbooks, and is a regular contributor to "Highlights for Children." Tom lives in Oak Park, Illinois.